THE
BLACK-FOOTED
FERRET

By Alvin and Virginia Silverstein
and Laura Silverstein Nunn

THE MILLBROOK PRESS, BROOKFIELD, CONNECTICUT

FOR CORY MICHAEL NUNN

The authors would like to thank Larry R. Shanks, Chief of Endangered Species
and Environmental Contaminants, U.S. Fish and Wildlife Service, for his enthusiasm
and help, for his careful reading of the manuscript and insightful suggestions, and
for the wealth of background material that he provided.

Cover photograph courtesy of Steve Kaufman/Peter Arnold, Inc.

Photographs courtesy of LuRay Parker © 1995 Wyoming Game & Fish Dept.: pp. 6, 14,
17, 26, 39, 41, 43, 45, 54; Dean Biggins, National Biological Survey, U.S. Dept. of the
Interior: pp. 8, 21, 25, 36, 47, 48; Peter Arnold, Inc.: pp. 18 (© R. Andrew Odun); U.S.
Fish and Wildlife Service: p. 33; Craig Flentie, Montana Black-Footed Ferret Recovery
Project, Montana Dept. of Fish, Wildlife & Parks: p. 52; Map by Joe LeMonnier.

Library of Congress Cataloging-in-Publication Data

Silverstein, Alvin.
The black-footed ferret / by Alvin and Virginia Silverstein
and Laura Silverstein Nunn.
p.   cm.—(Endangered in America)
Includes bibliographical references (p.   ) and index.
ISBN 1-56294-552-1
Summary: Traces the near-extinction of this prairie animal and the work
of the governmental agencies and wildlife biologists to protect it.
1. Black-footed ferret—Juvenile literature.   2. Endangered species—West (U.S.)
—Juvenile literature.   [1. Black-footed ferret.   2. Ferret.   3. Endangered species.]
I. Silverstein, Virginia B.   II. Nunn, Laura Silverstein.   III. Title.   IV. Series:
Silverstein, Alvin. Endangered in America.
QL737.C25S548   1995   333.95′9—dc20   94-44676   CIP   AC

CONTENTS

THE BLACK-FOOTED FERRET

A black-footed ferret in the wild.

THE MASKED BANDIT

The black-footed ferret is a small mammal with a "mask" of dark fur around its eyes. Some people think these facial markings are very appropriate. Like masked bandits, black-footed ferrets slink about at night, slipping in and out of prairie dog burrows in search of their prey. These nighttime hunters are so secretive that they are hard to spot—even by scientists looking for them in places where black-footed ferrets are known to be living. This is one important reason why no one is sure exactly how many once lived on the prairies of North America. It is also the main reason why no one realized that this species was in desperate danger until it was nearly too late to save it.

PART OF THE OLD WILD WEST

Native Americans were long aware of the black-footed ferret's close link to prairie dogs. In fact, the Sioux name for the ferret actually means "black-faced prairie dog." The Pawnees, whose legends described these animals

Like a masked bandit, the black-footed ferret slips in and out of prairie dog burrows.

as "staying hidden all the time," believed they had special powers. So did the Crows, who used them for sacred ceremonies and for medical rituals. The Cheyennes, Blackfeet, and Sioux used ferret furs to make their headdresses, and the Sioux used ferret hide as a sacred object in tribal ceremonies.

European settlers had been moving westward for quite some time before they became aware of black-footed ferrets. The species was first reported to the American public in 1851 by the famous artist and naturalist John James Audubon and his friend the Reverend John Bachman. Actually, they observed only one black-footed ferret skin, given to them by a trapper, and had trouble convincing people that the animal even existed because no more ferrets were spotted for another twenty-five years.

Black-footed ferrets may have been rather plentiful in the Great Plains during pioneer times, but since then they have faced a long, hard struggle to survive. Their problems began when settlers started turning the open plains into farms and ranches. Prairie dogs, the ferrets' main food source, had lived in huge "towns" of branching underground tunnels. But the new settlers considered them a nuisance. Prairie dogs were declared the number one enemy by farmers and ranchers. They claimed that these rodents were eating the vegetation meant for their livestock, and that their cattle and horses were stepping into prairie dog burrows and getting injured.

BIG CHANGES—AND UNINTENDED VICTIMS

The farmers and ranchers convinced the federal government to help them, and prairie dog control programs were started. In these programs, which became more popular in the early 1900s, poisoned baits were set out to kill off prairie dogs. Gradually the numbers of prairie dogs decreased, and many of their underground towns on the plains became deserted. But poisoning prairie dogs affected a whole chain of wildlife. Coyotes, foxes, and birds of prey had a harder time finding enough to eat. Many of them died. Black-footed ferrets suffered most of all, because prairie dogs had been their main source of food.

BELATED CONCERN

By the 1960s people were finally realizing that the black-footed ferret was in serious trouble. It was declared an endangered species, entitled to special protection, but still its numbers dropped. By 1972 many experts thought the species had become extinct. In 1981, though, a small population of black-footed ferrets was discovered in Meeteetse, Wyoming. But in 1984 an outbreak of disease swept through the little group; by 1985 most of the ferret population had been wiped out.

That year, wildlife biologists took a bold and desperate step. The Wyoming Game and Fish Department and the U.S. Fish and Wildlife Service (FWS) captured the last eighteen black-footed ferrets and placed them in a captive breeding facility. It was hoped that someday their descendants could be reintroduced into the wild.

Very little was known about black-footed ferrets at that time, and scientists had to learn quickly how to raise and breed them. An earlier breeding attempt had been a dismal failure, but with a lot of hard work by dedicated people, this one succeeded. Now, with the help of agencies and zoos, black-footed ferrets are being bred at a number of facilities in various parts of the country, and young ferrets are being released each year in several prairie states.

People brought black-footed ferrets to the edge of extinction, and there are still many threats to their existence in the wild. But with the enthusiastic help of scientists and nature lovers, these endearing animals have a good chance to live wild again.

WHAT IS THE BLACK-FOOTED FERRET?

The black-footed ferret belongs to the weasel family, *Mustelidae*, which includes weasels, minks, otters, skunks, martens, fishers, and wolverines. The family name comes from the Latin word for weasel, *mustela*; in fact, the black-footed ferret's scientific name, *Mustela nigripes*, literally means "black-footed weasel." It is the largest North American weasel, and it was once found over most of the prairies of the central and western United States—from Texas, Arizona, and New Mexico all the way up to Montana and Wyoming and even parts of Alberta and Saskatchewan, Canada.

WHAT DOES IT LOOK LIKE?

The black-footed ferret has a typically weasel-like body, long and slender. Adult males grow to about 20 to 24 inches (51 to 61 centimeters) long, including a 5- or 6-inch (13- or 15-centimeter) -long tail, but weigh only about 2 pounds (0.9 kilogram). By comparison, a housecat with a similar body length may weigh about 10 pounds (4.5 kilograms). Female black-footed ferrets are usually about 10 percent smaller than males. The ferret's slender shape is perfect for its way of life, slinking in and out of prairie dog burrows and slithering easily through their long, branching tunnels. Aboveground it can move quickly too, in long, loping bounds.

The ferret's short, sleek fur is a yellowish-buff color, lighter on the underparts and brown on the top of the head and middle of the back. Its most striking feature is a dark mask across the face, much like that of a raccoon. It also has black feet and legs, and a black tip on the tail.

THE FERRET FAMILY TREE

The black-footed ferret looks very similar to the fitch ferret, which is sold in pet stores. (The main difference is that the fitch ferret's tail is entirely black.) The fitch ferret is a close relative of the black-footed ferret. Both

An Old Relationship

FERRETS may seem like trendy, exotic pets today, but the European species is just as domesticated as cats and dogs. Pet ferrets were common in ancient Rome and often used for hunting rabbits and other burrowing animals. A trace of this old custom can be found in the common phrase "to ferret out," meaning to search out some hidden secret. The ferret's name comes from a Latin word for a thief.

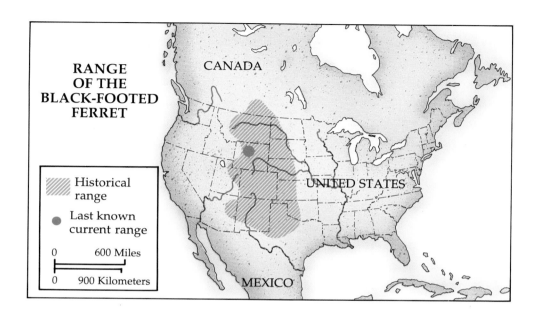

**RANGE
OF THE
BLACK-FOOTED
FERRET**

CANADA

UNITED STATES

MEXICO

Historical
range

Last known
current range

| 0 | 600 Miles |
| 0 | 900 Kilometers |

belong to the weasel family, but the domesticated fitch ferret came from
Europe, whereas the endangered black-footed ferret is native to North
America. The European ferret's scientific name is *Mustela putorius furo*.

Another close relative of the black-footed ferret is the Siberian polecat (*Mustela eversmanni*), from the great plains of Asia. These two species
are so closely related that they can even interbreed. Scientists believe that
Siberian polecats were the ancestors of black-footed ferrets. Long ago, a
land bridge connected Siberia and Alaska, and a number of animals (and
early humans) crossed over from northern Asia to North America. As the
ancestral polecats migrated to the American Great Plains, they gradually
changed. The animals best suited to the new environment passed on their
traits to their offspring, and eventually evolved into today's black-footed
ferret.

Black-footed ferrets hunt mainly at night, although they sometimes come out during the day. (Females who are hunting to feed their young are the most likely to be active during the daytime.) The ferrets can catch a variety of small animals, such as rabbits, rodents, insects, small birds, and even small snakes. But they prefer prairie dogs, which typically make up 90 percent of their diet.

The black-footed ferret's keen senses are a big help in its success as a hunter. Its dark eyes have sharp night vision. A reflecting layer at the back

The eyes of a black-footed ferret have a special layer that magnifies moonlight. This and the ferret's other sharp senses help it successfully hunt its prey at night.

of its eyeballs helps to magnify the faintest starlight or moonlight, providing a clear view of the ferret's surroundings. (In the beam of a flashlight, a black-footed ferret's eyes glow bright green as the light is reflected off this special layer.)

Keen hearing and a highly sensitive nose also help the ferret to find its prey and avoid enemies during its nighttime prowls. Its round ears quickly perk up at the slightest sound in the distance. It sniffs the air, using its sense of smell to locate food and detect danger. Scent helps to guide it to prairie dogs sleeping inside their burrows.

Members of the mustelid family are all equipped with scent or musk glands beneath their tails. The skunk, for example, is famous for its powerful odor. The musk glands of the black-footed ferret produce a more subtle scent, which it often leaves as a mark on bushes and trees. These marks announce the ferret's presence to other ferrets that might pass by.

THE BLACK-FOOTED FERRET'S LIFE

Winter can be fierce on the prairies, and some animals survive by hibernating. Some prairie dogs, for example, sleep away the winter snug in their burrows. Their heartbeat and breathing rates slow down, and their body temperature falls. With the body "thermostats" turned down this way, a hibernating animal does not use much energy, and the fat stored in its body will be enough to last it until spring.

Black-footed ferrets do not hibernate, though. They are active all winter, going out in the rain and snow. Even temperatures as low as $-36°F$ ($-37.7°C$) and winds up to 30 miles (48 kilometers) an hour do not faze them. They roam about, sometimes covering more than 4 miles (6 kilometers) in a single night, in search of food. When the ferret finds a prairie dog burrow, it may dig down into it, making a long, keyhole-shaped trench. After killing a prairie dog, it may drag the victim back to its burrow to eat underground.

Black-footed ferrets are good enough diggers to make their own burrows, but generally they make their homes in the empty burrows of prairie dogs. These cozy homes include branching tunnels with sleeping and resting chambers and, often, several entrance and exit holes.

A litter usually has four to six kits.

During the fall and winter, black-footed ferrets usually live alone, but by March or April they are ready to find a mate. Once the female becomes pregnant, the male's job is done. He continues to live his solitary life, while the female prepares to take care of the baby ferrets, known as kits, on her own.

KITS LEARN HOW TO HUNT

About six weeks after mating, the female black-footed ferret gives birth to a litter of four to six kits. The mother cares for her young inside the prairie dog burrow. She nurses them and brings them food every chance she gets. Sometimes she moves the kits around in different shelters so she can be close to her hunting grounds. She may even bring them to a burrow where she has left a freshly killed prairie dog. They begin to nibble at the food and learn to recognize the scent of their prey.

The kits normally stay underground until they are about six weeks old. When they are mature enough to come out of the burrow, their mother lets them tag along while she goes on her hunt. She tries to teach her young how to hunt down a prairie dog. On their first hunting trip, the kits are shy and scared. Their mother helps them until they catch on.

Kits soon learn to hide in the nearest prairie
dog burrow when danger approaches.

KITS LEARN THE BASICS FOR SURVIVAL

Hunting skills are not the only things black-footed ferret kits need to learn in order to survive in the wild. They must also be prepared to escape or defend themselves if they are faced with enemies. Although the ferrets are predators that live by hunting, they in turn are hunted by other predators, such as badgers, coyotes, and birds of prey.

When danger appears, the mother ferret tries to protect her young and begins hissing like a cat. If she feels threatened, she may bark wildly. The frightened kits scoot for the nearest hole and dive down into a prairie dog burrow to hide out until the danger passes. In most cases this gives them their best chance to survive, and the kits quickly learn to bolt for a hideout at the first sign of danger.

Predators are only one of the threats to the survival of black-footed ferrets in the wild. The ferrets are susceptible to various diseases, such as canine distemper, plague, and pneumonia. Distemper is a disease common among dogs, and black-footed ferrets can catch it too. But distemper is much more serious in ferrets and is nearly always fatal.

Kits who escape the threats of predators and disease grow quickly. By the fall the young ferrets are ready to live on their own. They leave their mother's burrow and move to other parts of the prairie dog town.

PRAIRIE DOG TOWN

When young ferrets begin life alone, they find a home burrow near an active prairie dog "town"—a group of burrows that may cover an area of 1 to 1,000 acres (0.4 to 405 hectares). Prairie dogs dig their large, branching burrows themselves. Their short, muscular front legs and long claws make good digging tools. Typically, the entrance hole leading into each burrow is surrounded by a dome-shaped mound, produced by the dirt thrown out during the digging of the tunnels. Like squirrels, prairie dogs often sit up on their hind feet in order to have a wider view of the land, watching out for possible predators. Besides ferrets, their enemies include various other wild animals and humans.

Prairie dog towns may have as many as fifty burrow entrances per acre. The largest prairie dog town ever found, in Texas, was 100 miles (160 kilometers) wide and 250 miles (400 kilometers) long, with a population estimated at 400 million!

Prairie dogs are the black-footed ferret's preferred source of food and their burrows the ferret's favorite habitat.

Natural boundaries, such as ridges, lines of trees, and roads, divide large prairie dog towns into smaller sections called wards. These wards are divided into a number of coteries, or private groups. Coteries typically consist of one adult male, three adult females, and four young ones.

A Prairie Dog Family Tree

IN 1742 two French explorers, Louis and François Vérendrye, observed squirrel-like animals on the western plains. When the little animals spotted the explorers, they stood up and gave out yipping barks, then dove into their burrows. The Frenchmen named the animals *"petits chiens,"* or little dogs. They became known as black-tailed prairie dogs.

Prairie dogs belong to the *Sciuridae*, or squirrel, family. They live on the grasslands, or prairies, located in the Great Plains in the western United States. There are five species, or kinds, of prairie dogs. The largest and most common are the black-tailed prairie dogs, named for the black tips on their tails. They were once found throughout the Great Plains, from northern Mexico to southern Canada. An adult black-tailed prairie dog weighs 1 to 3 pounds (0.5 to 1.4 kilograms) and is 14 to 17 inches (36 to 43 centimeters) in length. The somewhat smaller Mexican prairie dogs also have black-tipped tails. They are found only in Mexico and are an endangered species. White-tailed prairie dogs and Gunnison's prairie dogs, which live on high plateaus, have white-tipped tails. So do Utah prairie dogs, a threatened species found only in that state.

The coterie is the center of the prairie dog's life. It is the family unit, with its own territory (usually about an acre), which it defends against strangers. Prairie dogs rarely leave their coterie, and if they do they are promptly chased out by members of neighboring coteries. If the stranger refuses to leave, the adult male of the coterie comes out to defend his territory. Usually such disputes consist mainly of bluffing, with each male taking threatening poses. But sometimes, when the newcomer is looking for mates or trying to expand his territory, the two males fight. The loser of the fight is forced to leave the area.

Members of a single coterie are very close and affectionate toward one another. They often spend time grooming each other. They also greet each other with little kisses as a sign of welcome.

The daytime is the active time for prairie dogs. They get up when the sun rises and go out to feed on grasses and other greens. In the summer it is too hot in the middle of the day (more than 100°F, or 38°C), so the prairie dogs take a noontime siesta in their cool burrows, then come out to feed again in the afternoon. Black-tailed prairie dogs are active all year round. They may stay inside for a few days during the worst winter storms, but on nice days they come out in the afternoon to bask in the winter sun. The other prairie dog species live at higher elevations where the winters are more severe. These prairie dogs fatten up in the late summer and early fall, then hibernate from October to the end of February, living on their reserves of body fat.

PREPARING FOR DANGER

Although members of nearby coteries rarely interact with each other, the boundaries quickly disappear when danger approaches. The first prairie dog to spot a predator, such as a coyote, lets out a high-pitched bark to

Inside a Prairie Dog Burrow

THE ENTRANCE of a prairie dog burrow leads into a 15-foot (5-meter) -long tunnel that goes down 6 feet (2 meters) deep or more. There may be a small chamber dug out just below the surface, where the prairie dogs can sit and listen for noises above. In the deeper parts of the burrow there are nest chambers for sleeping and raising the young. The dome-shaped entrance mounds make good lookout stations, and they also help to keep the burrows from flooding when it rains.

warn all the others in the prairie dog town. Members of nearby coteries quickly scatter to their burrows. Some stand on the entrance mounds and join the barking chorus before diving for safety. Then they wait underground. As soon as the danger is gone, a brave prairie dog gives an all-clear barking call, and things return to normal.

Coyotes, bobcats, and foxes hunt prairie dogs and other small animals mainly when these animals are out feeding among the grasses. Or the predator may sit at the entrance of a burrow, waiting patiently for an unlucky prairie dog to come out. Hawks and eagles soar over the prairie dog town and swoop down if they spot their prey. Rattlesnakes may eat young prairie dogs, but they usually don't bother the adults. Badgers, which can dig into burrows after prairie dogs or rabbits, are a more serious threat. And so are weasels and ferrets, which are slim enough to wriggle down into the burrows and fierce enough to kill prey that is larger than they are.

The dome-shaped entry mounds to prairie dog
burrows serve as lookout stations.

The ferret's long, slim shape is perfectly suited
for slipping into prairie dog burrows.

THERE'S NO ESCAPING THE BLACK-FOOTED FERRET

Seeking refuge in the burrows usually protects the prairie dogs from most of their enemies, but not from the resourceful black-footed ferret. Slipping into prairie dog burrows is an easy task for the ferret. It does most of its hunting at night, when prairie dogs are asleep. To protect themselves while they sleep, some prairie dogs try to reinforce their burrows with dirt to keep out the intruders. But it doesn't take the ferret long to dig its way into the burrow. A quick bite on the neck kills its sleeping prey. But if the prairie dogs are awake, the ferret's task is much harder. An adult prairie dog is as large as a ferret, or even larger. When the ferret attacks, the prairie dog may fight back, biting with its sharp front teeth until it has a chance to get away. Many ferrets in the wild have scars from fights with prairie dogs.

THE BATTLE WITH HUMANS

Humans have turned out to be the prairie dog's worst enemy. Since the 1800s, ranchers and farmers have campaigned against these rodents. They claim that prairie dogs ruin grazing land by eating the grass right down to the ground, and thus take food that could have been used by cattle. They point out that prairie dog burrows are a hazard to both cattle and horses, which can step into a hole and break a leg. Rattlesnakes and black widow spiders, which often make their homes in abandoned prairie dog burrows, are also hazards to people who walk on the prairies.

Prairie dogs can also harbor a dangerous disease, plague, caused by a bacterium called *Yersinia pestis* and transmitted by the bites of infected fleas. In the Middle Ages this disease, called the "black death," wiped out one third of the population of Europe. But with today's medical tests and treatments, plague is rare and usually curable. It is far more serious in rodents. Outbreaks of plague can sweep rapidly through a prairie dog town and wipe out whole colonies.

Is the Prairie Dog Really a Pest?

WILDLIFE BIOLOGISTS today believe that prairie dogs don't really ruin grazing lands. Instead, they tend to spread into areas that have already been seriously overgrazed by cattle and actually help to repair the damage. In digging their burrows, prairie dogs help to mix the soil. By eating grasses down close to the soil line, they stimulate new growth—and the new growth has a higher nutritional value for grazing animals. Some studies show that the weight gain of cattle and buffalo that graze on prairie dog areas is just as good as or even better than that on lands where the "pests" have been exterminated. Moreover, prairie dog towns attract a rich variety of wildlife. Empty burrows provide homes for rabbits, burrowing owls, and other wildlife species. Buffalo, mule deer, elk, and antelope may come to graze on the rich plant life. Songbirds are attracted by the wealth of seeds and insects. In one study, more than 140 different species of wildlife were found to be associated with prairie dog towns.

PRAIRIE DOG CONTROL PROGRAMS

Sympathetic congressmen listened to the complaints of the prairie settlers. Soon the federal and state governments were setting up plans to control the prairie dog "pest" problem. The first official program to control the prairie dog populations was created in the late 1800s. Control programs became more popular in the 1900s, reaching a peak just after World War II. Various methods were used to exterminate prairie dogs, such as shooting, dynamiting, and gassing the burrows, but the most effective method was poisoning. The government distributed a potent poison called Compound 1080. Ranchers mixed this poison into grains and spread it over millions of acres of prairie dog colonies. The problem with Compound 1080, however, is that this poison does not break down in the body of its victim, so any animal that feeds on the carcass may also be poisoned. A ferret that ate a sick or dead prairie dog poisoned by Compound 1080 could also die from the poison. Therefore, the prairie dogs were not the only targets hit by this control program.

In 1972, Compound 1080 was no longer considered effective, and the control programs switched to using strychnine. By the 1970s nearly 98 million acres (40 million hectares) once inhabited by prairie dogs had been poisoned, reducing the prairie dog population by 95 percent since the beginning of the twentieth century. In some areas prairie dogs have been eliminated completely. But prairie dogs were a key part of the prairie ecology. Their disappearance has led to declines in a number of other wild animals, such as burrowing owls and swift foxes, dangerously upsetting the balance of nature. Unfortunately, these control programs were begun—and continue today in some places—without any serious thought to their consequences.

ON THE ROAD TO EXTINCTION

The plants and animals of a wildlife community are joined together in a complex web of relationships, formed by interlinking food chains. Plants grow in the soil or water, producing food substances from raw materials provided by the air, water, and soil. Animals feed on the plants, and they, in turn, are eaten by other animals. The prairie food chain involving the black-footed ferret has five main links, each of which is important in helping to maintain the balance of nature.

THE PRAIRIE FOOD CHAIN

The first link is the prairie grass, which is eaten by prairie dogs and other rodents—the second link. These grass consumers become the prey of predators such as the black-footed ferret—the third link in the food chain. But the ferrets, in turn, are preyed upon by other predators, such as coyotes, badgers, and birds of prey—the fourth link in the chain. When a coyote dies on the prairie, its body may become food for scavengers, such as beetles and ants, and be broken down by bacteria into minerals and other chemicals. In this fifth link in the food chain, chemicals are returned to the prairie soil, where they provide nourishment for plants and start the cycle again.

A natural wildlife community has many such food chains. If one link is lost, the higher links that depended on it may find enough substitutes to survive. Coyotes, for example, may eat mice or rabbits or a variety of other small animals. But the loss of a key link can be devastating for specialists like the black-footed ferret.

WAS THE BLACK-FOOTED FERRET EXTINCT?

The disappearance of the prairie dog affected black-footed ferrets in several ways. As their main food source became scarce, many young ferrets did not get enough food to survive or to breed. The survivors had to spread out to find food, but this made it difficult for them to find mates. Those that were able to mate formed small, isolated populations. In these small groups, it was likely that mates would be close relatives. In such cases, which scientists call inbreeding, it is reasonable to assume that parents will have many genes in common, and thus their offspring will get a "double dose" of the genes determining various traits. There may be a danger in this, because some genes result in birth defects or an increased susceptibility to disease. Such a defective gene may not cause trouble for most of a population, because there is also a normal gene that cancels out its effects. But inbred animals are more likely to inherit defective genes from both parents, making the population less able to survive.

Concerned naturalists had been predicting trouble for black-footed ferrets for a long time. Ferdinand V. Hayden, who mapped the Colorado

Rockies, had reported in 1877 that the species was "not at all rare." But by the early 1900s naturalist Ernest Thompson Seton wrote that the black-footed ferret "wears the mask of the death house" and warned that the species was in danger of extinction. In 1954 wildlife biologist Victor Cahalane described all of the recent ferret observations and pointed out how dangerously few there were. By the 1960s, out of about 130 U.S. counties and Canadian provinces where black-footed ferrets had been found since 1880, only *ten* still had living black-footed ferrets. And the situation continued to get worse. It was getting harder to find any ferrets at all!

In 1964 a small population of black-footed ferrets was discovered in South Dakota. Realizing that this might be their last chance, biologists began an intensive study that lasted for more than ten years. They located more than ninety ferrets, but this population was spread out over an area of about 7,700 square miles (19,900 square kilometers). Many deformities and cancers were observed among the South Dakota ferrets, apparently the result of inbreeding. By 1971 the numbers of this small group were dropping sharply, and no black-footed ferrets had been found anywhere else for a long time. So the Fish and Wildlife Service captured six of the animals and took them to the Patuxent Wildlife Research Center in Laurel, Maryland. This well-meaning attempt to help the species survive turned into a disaster.

At the time, no one knew very much about the biology and habits of black-footed ferrets. It was known that they were susceptible to canine distemper, so the first thing the researchers did was to inoculate the animals with a distemper vaccine. But they used too high a dose, and four of the ferrets died! Over the next few years, three more ferrets were captured in South Dakota and added to the little captive colony. But they did not reproduce successfully, and the last South Dakota ferret died in captivity in 1979.

$10,000 REWARD

FOR PHOTOGRAPH OR INFORMATION WHICH RESULTS IN VERIFICATION OF ONE OR MORE LIVE BLACK-FOOTED FERRETS

DO
NOT
KILL
OR
TRAP

Upper two black-footed ferrets by Dean Biggins. Ferret with prairie dog kill by Tim Clark. Ferret digging by Louise Forrest.

WANTED ALIVE
Black-footed ferrets and their locations

"Wanted" poster for any evidence that black-footed ferrets were still living in the wild.

Meanwhile, no one could find black-footed ferrets living wild. In 1967 the species was officially added to the endangered list. In the early 1970s biologist Tim Clark began putting up "WANTED" posters all over Wyoming, offering a $250 reward for anyone who could provide information leading to the discovery of black-footed ferrets in that state. But years went by, and no one claimed the reward. In 1978 a small population was discovered near Ekalaka, Montana, but those ferrets soon died out. It was beginning to look as though the black-footed ferret was gone forever.

A REPRIEVE FOR THE BLACK-FOOTED FERRET

By 1980, experts at the U.S. Fish and Wildlife Service were beginning to think that the black-footed ferret should be declared extinct. But Thomas Lovejoy, then with the World Wildlife Fund, thought it was too soon to write off the species. He got funding from Wildlife Preservation Trust International and expert help from the National Zoo and enlisted ecologist John Messick to search for ferrets in the western states. During the summer of 1981, Messick traveled through six states, talking to game wardens and other local people who might have spotted a black-footed ferret. He didn't find any ferrets, but one of the people he talked to was a taxidermist in Meeteetse, Wyoming.

Later that year, on a ranch near Meeteetse, a dog killed an animal that was taking food from its food dish. When it trotted home with the dead animal in its mouth, the rancher, John Hogg, threw the chewed-up carcass away. But his wife, Lucille, had noticed that the animal had unusual markings and wondered what it was. It looked something like a mink, but not like any mink she had ever seen. On her next trip into town, she carried the dead animal in a paper bag to the local taxidermy shop. Remembering his talk with John Messick, the taxidermist contacted the Wyoming Game and Fish Department. Game warden Jim Lawrence picked up the animal and sent it off to the U.S. Fish and Wildlife Service's Denver Wildlife Research Center in Fort Collins, Colorado. Sure enough, it was a black-footed ferret.

After identifying the animal, a team of researchers examined the body and found that the ferret had been plump and healthy when it was killed. So somewhere in Wyoming there must be a thriving black-footed ferret colony. The FWS team arranged a public meeting in Meeteetse, to discuss the find with local ranchers and townspeople. They presented a slide show on the ferrets and asked if anyone had seen an animal that looked like that. A ranch hand at a local ranch said he had recently seen one in a white-tailed prairie dog town about 3 miles (5 kilometers) from the Hoggs' ranch.

The ranch hand led the wildlife biologists to the prairie dog town, and the search began. On the first day the scientists didn't spot any ferrets, but they found ferret tracks in the snow and ferret scat (droppings). On their next trip they saw a ferret coming out of a prairie dog hole early one October morning. They set a tubular trap near the hole, and eleven hours later they caught a healthy young male ferret. A veterinarian anesthetized the ferret, and the scientists weighed and measured it, then fitted it with a collar carrying a small radio transmitter. After the ferret recovered from the anesthetic, it was released at the spot where it had been captured.

Over the next two weeks, biologists stayed at the site around the clock, monitoring the radio signals from the ferret's collar and observing it with spotting scopes and binoculars whenever it was above ground. While it was underground, they measured the movements they had mapped and searched for ferret tracks and scat. They mapped out the prairie dog burrows in the area and recorded which ones the ferret had

Black-footed ferret at Meeteetse site.

used for its den and how long it stayed in each one. Finally the radio failed, and a few days later the biologists trapped the animal again to examine it and remove the collar. Although the hair under the collar was matted down, the ferret did not seem to have suffered any bad effects from wearing it. Meanwhile, spotlight searching of the area continued for another few weeks, until mid-December. The research team recorded thirty-seven separate ferret sightings and estimated that there were about ten ferrets living there.

Over the next few years, the ferret colony near Meeteetse thrived. By 1984 the population hit a peak of 130 ferrets, occupying thirty-seven prairie dog colonies spread over about 150 square miles (400 square kilometers). But then a double disaster struck. First an epidemic of plague struck the prairie dogs in the area. Although scientists didn't know at the time that black-footed ferrets were susceptible to plague, they did realize that the epidemic was a major threat—it was killing off a big fraction of the ferrets' food supply. The research team that had been observing the colony rushed in to help, dusting the burrows with insecticides to kill the fleas that carried the disease. But then came the second blow. In the summer, an epidemic of canine distemper swept through the black-footed ferrets. By July 1985, spotlight surveys found only fifty-eight ferrets. By that fall, a total of 150 ferrets had died. This was a sign to wildlife organizations that the black-footed ferrets at Meeteetse were in desperate need of help.

CAPTIVE BREEDING PROGRAMS

By the fall of 1985, the last known surviving black-footed ferret colony was very small. Wildlife biologists feared that this colony was too small to survive, even if there were no new disease epidemics to wipe the animals out. So the Fish and Wildlife Service and the Wyoming Game and Fish Department took a drastic step. They captured some of the remaining ferrets and set up a captive breeding program at the Sybille Wildlife Research Institute, a division of the Wyoming Game and Fish Department. This marked the beginning of organized efforts to breed black-footed ferrets and eventually reintroduce the offspring into the wild.

STARTING FROM SCRATCH

Tom Thorne, a black-footed ferret expert, was put in charge of the captive breeding program. Thorne hired Don Kwiatkowski, a veterinarian, to live at the facility and care for the captive ferrets. While ferret kits had been

**Donald Kwiatkowski prepares
to examine ferrets in a release cage.**

born at the Fish and Wildlife Service facility at Patuxent, none had survived in captivity. The Sybille research team had to develop their own methods as they learned more about the species. The program did not have a very promising beginning. Two of the captured ferrets were sick. Before the researchers realized that the animals were suffering from distemper, they had transmitted the disease to the other four ferrets—and all six died! The biologists captured six more from the Meeteetse colony, leaving only a few in the wild.

At the request of the Fish and Wildlife Service, the Captive Breeding Specialist Group of the International Union for the Conservation of Nature and Natural Resources sent in a "SWAT team" to advise the Sybille biologists on breeding methods and to help them draw up a long-term recovery plan. In addition to the black-footed ferrets, the researchers raised and bred Siberian polecats. This closely related species might provide valuable clues for breeding the endangered ferrets. Moreover, because Siberian polecats are a plentiful species, researchers could try out breeding techniques on them first, without having to worry about making fatal mistakes.

DISAPPOINTMENTS CAN BE LEARNING EXPERIENCES

In the spring of 1986 the researchers waited eagerly for the first births of black-footed ferrets in captivity. But the captives did not mate successfully. Meanwhile, the ferrets left in the wild produced two litters, with a total of ten young. The remaining animals in the wild were captured and added to the breeding colony, except for one who escaped the traps.

Don Kwiatkowski suggested that the constant presence of the research team might be upsetting the captive ferrets and preventing them from breeding. So, in 1987, the researchers worked out a new setup, constructing nest boxes and placing television monitors in the breeding rooms so that the ferrets could be watched without being disturbed. They handled the ferrets as little as possible, mainly for medical treatments. The animals were anesthetized before being handled, to reduce stress and to prevent them from becoming too accustomed to humans. To transfer a ferret to the cage of a potential mate, it was lured into a small, tunnel-shaped cage and carried in that.

Below-ground nesting boxes were tried as part of the captive breeding program that released black-footed ferrets back onto the prairie.

Another problem was that no one knew how to tell when a black-footed ferret was in heat. In the wild the male and female get together only when she is ready to mate. But the researchers had to guess when to put pairs of ferrets together. If they were too early, the ferrets sometimes fought instead of mating. If they were too late, they missed the female's short fertile period. The researchers studied European ferrets and Siberian polecats to learn more about ferret breeding cycles. With suggestions from the "SWAT team," they tinkered with the lighting conditions in the cage areas and added vitamin supplements to the ferrets' diet.

The last known black-footed ferret in the wild had been captured on February 28, 1987. (Trapping him took a determined effort by a biologist who stayed out at the Meeteetse site for three days and three nights straight.) This male, "Scarface," began the 1987 breeding season. Now the captive breeding program was the last hope for the species.

Because ferrets are nocturnal animals, the researchers had to stay up all night watching on the TV monitor to see what happened when a pair of ferrets were placed together. All the effort paid off. Eleven females mated, and in June two of them produced litters. This was a big milestone—the first captive births. The Wyoming Game and Fish Department sponsored a naming contest, and entries (including names like "Ferret Faucet") poured in from all over the world. But the ferret was not out of danger yet. Only seven of the kits born in 1987 survived.

SUCCESS AT LAST

Based on where the ferrets were caught in the wild, the researchers carefully worked out breeding pairs to minimize inbreeding as much as possible. The numbers of the captive colony began to grow steadily. In 1988 thirteen litters were born at the Sybille facility, and thirty-four of the kits survived. Ferrets can mate before they are a year old, so the young ferrets quickly helped to build the population. By 1989 the number of captive ferrets had risen to 118. That year the researchers used Siberian polecats as foster mothers for some of the ferret kits. But these ferrets had some trouble socializing with others of their species. The researchers were afraid that polecat-raised ferrets might be unable to mate because of their confused identity. So in 1990 four fostered kits were placed with other young black-footed ferrets as soon as they were weaned, to help them to

A young
black-footed
ferret—one of
the first bred
in captivity.

identify with their own kind. By 1991 the captive population had grown to over 300—from the original eighteen ferrets.

To protect the colony from being wiped out by an epidemic of canine disease or some other catastrophe, the captive population was divided starting in 1988, and some of the ferrets were sent to other breeding facilities. A number of zoos offered to set up ferret programs at their own expense. The zoo in Omaha, Nebraska, and the National Zoo in Front Royal, Virginia, were the first, followed in 1989 by zoos in Louisville, Kentucky, Colorado Springs, Colorado, and Phoenix, Arizona. In 1993 another ferret breeding facility was set up in Toronto, Canada. Meanwhile, the encouraging success of the breeding program allowed the researchers to make serious plans for reintroducing black-footed ferrets into the wild.

BACK TO THE WILD

The captive breeding program for black-footed ferrets has been a success. It has saved the species from almost certain extinction. But wildlife specialists do not consider a wild species really "saved" until members of the species are firmly established in wild habitats, living in as close to natural conditions as possible.

It is not always easy to reintroduce wildlife into their wild habitat. During the generations of captive breeding, animals may become accustomed to being fed and cared for by humans. They may no longer have the skills to get food for themselves, or the reflexes necessary to protect themselves from predators and other dangers. Therefore, well-designed captive breeding programs try to keep the contact between the animals and their caretakers to a minimum, so the animals will not become "tame." The wildlife specialists must also teach the animals some basic survival skills, before taking them back to the wild.

Black-footed ferrets have been multiplying in captivity since the late 1980s, but they started from such small numbers that the reintroduction teams could not afford to make too many mistakes. Still, they needed answers to a lot of questions. Would it be better to release the ferrets gradually, feeding them artificially for a while? Or should they just open the cages and let them go? Would they leave the cages on their own, or

A black-footed ferret taking its first steps into the wild.

would they stay close by, expecting to be fed? Would they have to be taught to hunt and to avoid predators, or would their natural instincts take over? A lot of trial and error would be needed to find the best answers. So the researchers tried out some of their ideas and techniques first on Siberian polecats. All the polecats used in the program were neutered. In that way, if any of them could not be recaptured after the tests, they would not be able to form their own population in the wild and compete with the native wildlife.

The researchers had a number of imaginative ideas for teaching ferrets survival skills. Brian Miller, from the Conservation and Research Center near Front Royal, Virginia, mounted the stuffed head and paws of a badger on a radio-controlled toy truck. When this "Robo-Badger" came near the young polecats, they were frightened and quickly ran and hid in a nearby burrow. But a few seconds later they popped out to look around again. Miller shot rubber bands at them with a toy gun. He hoped that being frightened this way would teach the kits to run away when they spotted a real badger. In another experiment a stuffed great horned owl was suspended from the ceiling on a fishing line and sent swooping over the polecat kits. This time they ran for cover and did not reappear.

Using Siberian polecats seemed like a bright idea, but the practice "reintroductions" did not work very well. Dozens of radio-collared Siberian polecats were released, but about a third of them were quickly gobbled up by badgers. Most of the rest were eaten by coyotes, and the few that escaped that fate were caught by night-hunting birds such as great horned owls. The special survival lessons helped a little—six of the first thirteen young polecats, which had received only a little training, were killed within two days after their release, whereas better-trained polecats released later survived for a few weeks. But that wasn't good enough. The main lesson the researchers learned from the polecat studies was to try to keep the captive black-footed ferrets as wild as possible.

CAPTIVE BLACK-FOOTED FERRETS HUNT SUCCESSFULLY

The results of the polecat experiments were used as a guide for the next stage, developing techniques for releasing black-footed ferrets. Starting in 1990, ferrets were placed in a large fenced-in enclosure in the midst of a thriving prairie dog town. This experiment had two main goals. First, the researchers wanted to observe how well captive-bred ferret kits could adapt to an outdoor environment similar to their natural habitat. The second goal was to evaluate the ferrets' hunting skills. The black-footed ferrets adjusted rather well to living in the prairie dog burrows. And they caught on quickly when it came to capturing and killing prairie dogs. So it seemed that the black-footed ferrets would be able to thrive in the wild if only they could escape their predators.

To teach young ferrets survival skills, researchers invented a "Robo-Badger."

BACK IN THE WILD

In 1991 the researchers were ready to try the real thing. That fall forty-nine animals were released in the Shirley Basin near Medicine Bow, Wyoming. Thirty-nine of them wore radio collars, enabling researchers to track their movements. In the early winter the biologists decided to remove the collars to give the ferrets the best chance to survive. Then they waited anxiously. There wasn't much snow that winter, so the research team could not use the easiest way of checking on wild ferrets—looking

A ferret is fitted with a radio collar.

for their tracks in the snow. Finally, in March 1992, there was a snowfall, and seven sets of ferret tracks were found. Eagerly the scientists waited for the result of a spotlight search in July, when any ferrets would probably be active—roaming about during the summer nights. They also hoped to spot ferret kits coming out of their dens.

These high hopes were not very realistic. Black-footed ferrets usually live no more than two years in the wild, and most of the kits born each year do not survive to have young of their own. Experts from the Fish and Wildlife Service estimated that the program could be considered a success if 20 percent of the animals released survived for at least one month, and half of those survivors lasted through the winter. Actually, the ferrets from the first release did better than that. Twelve of them were still alive after a month, and seven made it through the winter. In mid-July an adult ferret with two kits was spotted, and later another litter was found. The first year was a big success.

BUILDING ON SUCCESS

The wildlife team studied the results of the first release, trying to learn which techniques were the most successful and what mistakes had been made. They found that survival was the highest in the areas where the ferrets were left alone, with a minimum of radio monitoring, cage cleaning, feeding, and visits from media reporters and photographers. The ferrets that stayed near the release cage for a while, using it for shelter, also seemed better able to make it on their own in the wild.

These lessons were incorporated into the plans for the next year's release in Wyoming. The cages were not all placed in one area, as they had been in 1991, but instead were spaced out in groups of five to seven, about a quarter of a mile apart. All the animals were delivered at the same time, and—to encourage the ferrets to regard the cages as "home"—they were not reused for new releases later that year.

The cage design was changed too. The original release cages were rather similar to the cages in the captive breeding facility. The breeding cages were mounted on legs, to make cleaning and servicing easier, and they contained nest boxes on the floor, connected to the main cage and nest box by plastic tubing. The first release cages were also mounted on legs—to help protect the ferrets from badgers, which are not good climbers. Plastic tubing, too narrow for a badger to enter, hung down to the ground. The young ferrets, used to going up and down the tubing in their breeding cages, had no trouble with this arrangement. But in 1992 the researchers also tried ground-level release cages, with below-ground nest boxes. Although this arrangement seemed more natural for burrowing animals, the first few years of testing did not show a clear advantage for either type; so both continued to be used.

Meanwhile, black-footed ferrets continued to thrive in the captive breeding facilities, and it was decided to keep a population of about 300 in captivity and release all the extra animals into the wild. In 1994 the release program was expanded to two more sites, in Montana and South Dakota, and some new techniques were tried. For example, some animals spent the last part of their captive life in a "halfway house"—an indoor prairie dog town—before their release into the wild. Some ferret kits were even born in the "halfway house" and never realized they were living in captivity. It will take a few years to fully evaluate the new methods.

FUTURE OF THE BLACK-FOOTED FERRET

The black-footed ferret recovery program has been a success. Starting with practically no knowledge of the species' biology and habits in the mid-1980s, the dedicated wildlife research team moved to the reintroduction stage faster than in any other endangered species program. Once again, black-footed ferrets are living wild in parts of their old range. But the battle is still far from won. Their numbers are still so small that an active captive breeding and reintroduction program will be needed for many years to come.

This program has allowed the team members to take setbacks and disappointments in stride. And with a species so close to extinction as the black-footed ferret, there are bound to be plenty of rough spots along the way. In 1994, for example, researchers were stunned to count only five ferrets at the Shirley Basin site in Wyoming—down from a thriving population of twenty wild-living ferrets and fifty newcomers introduced the previous fall. Something had happened over the winter—perhaps another epidemic—to threaten the little ferret colony. But forty new ferrets were due to be added later in the year, and more born each year in the breeding facilities.

THE RECOVERY PLAN

How many wild black-footed ferrets will be needed to be sure the species can survive on its own? Wildlife biologists have estimated that about 200 breeding animals is the minimum for a sustainable population. (Since only about a third of the ferrets in a typical population are breeding animals, that means a total population of about 600 ferrets.) For a population to maintain itself indefinitely, without human help, about 500 breeding animals would be needed—a total of about 1,500 ferrets all

A biologist with the Montana Department of Fish, Wildlife and Parks releases the first black-footed ferret reintroduced into Montana.

together. That is the national goal set by the U.S. Fish and Wildlife Service: 1,500 wild-living black-footed ferrets, in ten populations spread throughout the former range of the species.

It has been estimated that each adult ferret needs a hunting territory of at least 100 acres (40 hectares). So more than 150,000 acres (60,700 hectares) of protected prairie dog country will be needed to reach the national goal. That may sound like a lot, but it is less than 0.01 percent of the public land in the West.

CAN WE REACH THE GOAL?

Black-footed ferrets have had one big advantage in the campaign to save them from extinction. They are cute and cuddly looking. Their alert faces with bright eyes and mischievous-seeming mask have captured the hearts of millions and have won over many people to the cause of helping endangered wildlife. But they face some big disadvantages too. In addition to the natural hazards of disease and predators, they are innocent bystanders in the path of humans who want to use the lands where they live.

Researchers are doing their part in the fight. Some are working out techniques to help in the captive breeding effort. With artificial insemination and the use of frozen sperm, eggs, and embryos, for example, even animals that are unable to breed successfully on their own can contribute their genes to the growing population.

Other researchers are developing better distemper vaccines. The killed-virus vaccines now being used provide protection for only ninety days. Live vaccines would provide longer-lasting protection—for two to three years, which is enough to cover the average black-footed ferret's

**Fifteen hundred black-footed ferrets living in the wild
is the goal set by the U.S. Fish and Wildlife Service.**

lifetime in the wild. But the live-virus vaccines tested weaken ferrets' defenses against other diseases for about a month after the vaccination. If they were given a live-virus vaccine right before release, they would be vulnerable to disease just at the time they were trying to adapt to their new surroundings. The vaccine cannot be given sooner because the ferrets are too young. (They are usually released at about fourteen weeks, when they are old enough to hunt on their own.) In the future, vaccines that can be added to bait eaten by wild animals may help to solve the problem. This kind of approach has helped to wipe out rabies in foxes in Europe and is being tested against the rabies epidemic in raccoons in the United States.

But the main obstacle to the successful return of the black-footed ferret is the insistence by farmers and ranchers on prairie dog control programs. While state and national wildlife services are pouring thousands of dollars into ferret recovery programs, other government agencies are spending even more money on programs to kill prairie dogs. From 1980 through 1984, for example, the Bureau of Indian Affairs spent $6.2 million to poison prairie dogs on 450,000 acres (180,000 hectares) in the Pine Ridge Indian Reservation near the Badlands National Park in South Dakota. That sum is far more than the market value of the livestock the program was supposed to protect, and even more than the value of the land itself! The National Farm Bureau and the U.S. Forest Service are also conducting expensive programs to wipe out prairie dogs.

In spite of studies showing that prairie dogs help repair overgrazed land, many people regard them as pests. South Dakota (where ferrets are being reintroduced) lists prairie dogs as pests, and the Colorado Department of Agriculture refers to grasslands "infested" by prairie dogs. There are laws in parts of Nebraska and Kansas *requiring* landowners who find prairie dogs on their property to exterminate them.

Although the Endangered Species Act mandates an effort to save black-footed ferrets from extinction, the practical problems of setting up recovery programs are often discouraging. In the early 1990s, for example, 500,000 acres (200,000 hectares) of national grasslands south of the Badlands National Park were slated for a prairie dog control effort. These lands were leased by a total of only eleven ranchers. But when the Fish and Wildlife Service requested that 20,000 acres (8,100 hectares) be set aside as a protected ferret reintroduction site, local meetings produced heated opposition. In the end, the FWS got only 5,000 acres (2,000 hectares), and the prairie dogs were wiped out on all the rest.

There are bright spots in the picture, however. Many landowners are cooperating with reintroduction programs, and publicity for the effort has brought help and support from the public. Dedicated volunteers aid in

Saved by an Exception

IRONICALLY, the success of ferret reintroduction programs has been helped by a decision to allow exceptions to the strict rules of the Endangered Species Act. This law makes it illegal to kill or injure any endangered animal, with stiff penalties for any offenders. Farmers and ranchers were reluctant to allow ferret refuges to be set up on or near their property, until the reintroduced animals were declared "nonessential." In the interest of saving the species, the wildlife biologists conceded that some individual animals need not be so strictly protected. Landowners are much more willing to cooperate with recovery programs when they do not have to fear being fined or sent to jail if they accidentally hurt a ferret.

the observation programs, and outside resources are adding funds to the government-sponsored efforts. In 1988, for example, the Chevron Corporation donated $5,000 toward the captive breeding programs. In addition, Chevron employees also donated $10,000 to the University of Wyoming to help support the reintroduction research.

The program got another boost in 1995 when funds totaling $200,000 were obtained from the U.S. Fish and Wildlife Service, the Wyoming Wildlife Agency and the National Wildlife Federation. An additional $50,000 contribution was also made by PIC Technologies, Inc., a Wyoming oil and gas company.

With friends like these, there is real hope that black-footed ferrets will regain their place in the wild.

FINGERTIP FACTS

Length	Average is 18 to 24 inches (46 to 61 centimeters) long, including a 5-inch (13-centimeter) tail.
Weight	Adult males weigh between 1.5 and 2.5 pounds (0.7 and 1.1 kilograms) (females are about 10 percent smaller).
Color	Yellowish-buff color on the body, a dark-colored mask across the face; black legs and feet, and a black tip on the tail.
Food	Primary food source is the prairie dog, but ferrets will eat insects, rabbits, rodents, squirrels, small birds, and small snakes.
Reproduction	Females are ready to breed just under a year old; most males are not ready to breed until their second year. They breed every spring, April or May; litter consists of 4 to 6 kits.
Care for young	The female takes full responsibility for her kits; she nurses and feeds them. She also teaches them how to hunt and to defend themselves against predators.

Range	They were once found in parts of Canada (Alberta and Saskatchewan), Montana, Wyoming, North Dakota, South Dakota, Nebraska, Utah, Colorado, Kansas, Arizona, New Mexico, Oklahoma, and Texas. Now limited to various captive breeding facilities and isolated reintroduction sites in Wyoming, South Dakota, and Montana.
Population size	Highly threatened; about 300 in captive breeding facilities and small numbers in reintroduction sites.
Social behavior	Solitary animals except during the mating season.
Life span	Can live up to 12 years in captivity, but only up to 5 to 6 years in the wild. (The average life span in the wild is only about 2 years.)

FURTHER READING

Books

Casey, Denise. *Black-footed Ferret*. New York: Dodd, Mead, 1985.

DeBlieu, Jan. *Meant to Be Wild*. Golden, Colo.: Fulcrum, 1991.

Field, Jay and Mary. *A Step-by-Step Book about Ferrets*. Neptune City, N.J.: T.F.H. Publications, 1987.

McNulty, Faith. *Must They Die?* Garden City, N.Y.: Doubleday, 1971.

Roever, J. M. *The Black-Footed Ferret*. Austin, Tex.: Steck-Vaughn, 1972.

Pamphlets

"Black-Footed Ferret (*Mustela nigripes*)," Endangered Species Biologue Series, U.S. Fish and Wildlife Service, August 1991.

"Black-Footed Ferret Recovery Plan," by Steven C. Forrest and Dean Biggins, U.S. Fish and Wildlife Service, August 8, 1988.

"The Montana Black-Footed Ferret Recovery Project," Montana Department of Fish, Wildlife and Parks, Bureau of Land Management, and U.S. Fish and

Wildlife Service, reprint of "The Ferret Experiment," *Montana Outdoors*, March-April 1992.

"Prairie Dogs and Their Ecosystem," by Nancy S. Foster and Scott E. Hygnstrom, University of Nebraska, Lincoln, Department of Forestry, Fisheries and Wildlife.

"Return of a Native: The Black-footed Ferret of the American Prairie," Wyoming Game and Fish Department, Bureau of Land Management, and U.S. Fish and Wildlife Service.

Articles

Chadwick, Douglas H. "Rescuing Our Rarest Prairie Predator," *Defenders*, March-April 1991, pp. 10–23.

Crane, Candace. "A Ferret Odyssey," *Wyoming Wildlife*, February 1991, pp. 26–33.

Crane, Candace. "The Ferrets That Wouldn't Die," *Animals*, May-June 1990, pp. 18–22.

Gibson, Jim. "International Ferrets?" *Wyoming Wildlife*, May 1989, pp. 16–21.

Gray, Mary Taylor. "The Future of Ferrets," *Colorado Outdoors*, January-February 1991, pp. 16–19.

Mulhern, Dan. "Return of the Masked Stranger," *Kansas Wildlife & Parks*, September-October 1989, pp. 41–44.

Nice, Joan. "Long Road to Recovery," *National Wildlife Federation*, June-July 1988, pp. 16–19.

Oakleaf, Bob. "First Spring," *Wyoming Wildlife*, June 1992, pp. 21–29.

Schroeder, Max. "The Black-Footed Ferret," *Audubon Wildlife Report 1987*, pp. 446–455.

Strickland, Dale. "Ferret Update," *Wyoming Wildlife*, March 1982, pp. 4–6.

Weinberg, Susan. "The Once and Future Ferret," *Zoogoer*, January-February 1989, pp. 4–7.

ORGANIZATIONS

Black-footed Ferret Fund
National Fish and Wildlife Foundation
18th and C Street NW, Room 2725, Washington, DC 20240

Bureau of Land Management
P.O. Box 36800, Billings, MT 59107
(406) 255-2913

Montana Fish, Wildlife and Parks
1420 East Sixth Avenue, Helena, MT 59620
(406) 444-2535

U.S. Fish and Wildlife Service
P.O. Box 25486, Denver Federal Center, Denver CO 80225
(393) 236-8676

Wyoming Game and Fish Department
5400 Bishop Boulevard, Cheyenne, WY 82006
(307) 777-4600

INDEX

Page numbers in *italics* refer to illustrations.

ABOUT THE AUTHORS

Alvin Silverstein is a
professor of biology at the
City University of New York,
College of Staten Island;
Virginia Silverstein, his wife, is
a translator of Russian scientific
literature. Together they have
published more than 100 books
on science and health topics.

Laura Silverstein Nunn, a graduate
of Kean College with a major in
sociology, has been helping with
the research for her parents' books
since her high school days and has
recently joined the Silverstein
writing team. She lives with her
husband Matt and baby son Cory in
a rural New Jersey town not far
from her childhood home.